Misty Morning at the race course

Saratoga

AN EQUINE TRADITION

TOM KILLIPS

Published by PMC
300 Fairfield Road
Fairfield, New Jersey 07004

Printed in the United States of America

First printing, 1996

ISBN: 1-881275-26-4

This book was printed and bound by Horowitz/ Rae Book Mfg. Co.

Book design and layout by Deborah L. Killips
Creative consultant: Thomas Antis
Technical adviser: Eileen Bonville

Dedication:

This book is dedicated to my mother, Nevada Killips. Always supportive of my work, she enthusiastically looked forward to the completion of this project.

Unfortunately, she died in January and never saw the finished book.

The manner in which she lived will always be remembered and will serve as a continual inspiration to me.

Tom

Introduction

The first time I visited Saratoga Springs, I was assigned to photograph the feature race at Saratoga Race Course. I parked on the grass beneath giant trees and walked through the historic wooden clubhouse feeling as if I had gone back in time. It was the first of what would become hundreds of visits to this famous track.

For the past 15 years, I have covered the opening day of the annual race meet. Perhaps because the meet lasts for only 34 days (it used to be 24), there is a special type of excitement on the first day. Familiar faces mix with the wealthy, the famous, and the not so famous in a setting typical of Saratoga.

It seems almost everyone saves their most outrageous or fashionable hat to wear at the track. Hat wearing has become such a tradition, there is even a "Hat Day" with contests for different style hats.

The preservation of so many traditions in a setting that seems impervious to change creates an enviroment unique to Saratoga. Everywhere you look, you find traditions meticulously maintained.

The row of jockey statues outside the Wright Street entrance are painted each year in the colors of the previous meet's Grade I stakes winners. Similarly, the canoe, which floats on the infield pond, is painted annually in the colors of the Travers Stakes winner.

The thoroughbreds are saddled beneath trees within a few feet of the crowd. An intimacy exists between the fans and the competitors in the paddock area unlike anywhere else in the world of sports.

My favorite tradition is breakfast at the track. There is almost a surreal feeling as you sit in the clubhouse watching the morning workouts. These magnificent 1,000 pound animals emerge from the mist, which so frequently blankets the track in August, snorting and billowing steam like creatures from a mythical story.

It is during the early morning hours that you can truly appreciate the dedication trainers and jockeys have for their chosen craft. They arrive at the stables in the darkness of the early morning and follow a regular routine to insure each horse is properly trained. Some of the most fascinating people can be found on the backstretch early in the day.

In the afternoon the atmosphere at the track is completely different. The attention shifts to the tote board and every type of person imaginable attempts to handicap each race and beat the odds. Saratoga accomodates all the fans by providing a varied race card each day, including steeplechase races.

The evening polo matches have increasingly become a significant part of the summer experience. It is common to see people having a picnic "tailgate" style along one side of the field, while a gala takes place beneath the tents on the "members only" side of the field. Between chukkers, people from both sides mingle on the field as they help to replace the sod torn loose by the sharp turns and sudden stops of the polo ponies.

After the matches it is on to the Saratoga Raceway, just a short drive down Nelson Avenue from the thoroughbred track, for a night of harness racing on one of the country's fastest half mile oval tracks. This type of racing most closely resembles the first races ever contested in Saratoga, where horses pulled carriages, rather than being ridden.

Harness racing takes place nine months a year. Watching the morning workouts as the horses run past snow covered trees in early March is very different from the thoroughbred's August workouts. Yet, both are part of the Saratoga equine scene, which helps make this community unique.

The variety of equine activity that extends beyond the summer months includes dressage at the race course, St. Clement's Horse Show at the Oklahoma training track, and carriage driving competitions at the Raceway. Carriages can be seen almost anytime transporting people to special events. Saratoga has truly become a year-round equine center.

Appropriately, Skidmore College, located on North Broadway, fields one of the finest intercollegiate riding teams in the country. They won the national riding title in 1995 and successfully defended it in 1996. Frequently, they host horse shows at their riding center.

While the breadth and scope of equine activity continues to grow, the busiest month is still August. So much action is packed in this one month the city virtually bursts at the seams. Thousands of people visit each year and there seem to be an endless stream of fund-raising galas, luncheons, and other events that come with the annual thoroughbred meet.

The highlight is always Travers Week. A week that includes a parade, a ball, and the running of the oldest graded stakes race in the United States. This year will mark the 127th running of the Travers. This race embodies much of the history and tradition associated with the Saratoga Race Course.

Part of that history is Saratoga's reputation as the "graveyard of favorites". A perfect example was the 1930 Travers Stakes race where **Jim Dandy** , a 100-1 longshot defeated Triple Crown winner **Gallant Fox**. Today, that historic moment is commemorated by a race named after **Jim Dandy**. The Jim Dandy Stakes runs two weeks before the Travers and serves as a prep race for many Travers entries.

Saratoga Springs is not only a haven for horse lovers it is also a favorite place for artists. The equine activity and the extraordinary mix of people interacting in a setting rich in tradition and history create the perfect atmosphere for artists and photographers.

On the pages that follow, I am proud to share with you some of the special people and events it has been my pleasure to photograph during these past 16 years.

Steaming thoroughbred

Thunder Rumble wins
the Saratoga Cup, 1994

Rooftop view of the start

Racing past the clubhouse

Woody Stevens, Hall of Fame trainer

Morning workouts on the race course backstretch

Dinwitty Lampton and Marylou Whitney arriving at the track

Carriages parade past the clubhouse

Mercedes Benz

High goal polo match

All eyes are on the stretch run.

Corporate Report (right) wins the 1991 Travers.

Practice jumping at Skidmore College

Winter workouts at the harness track

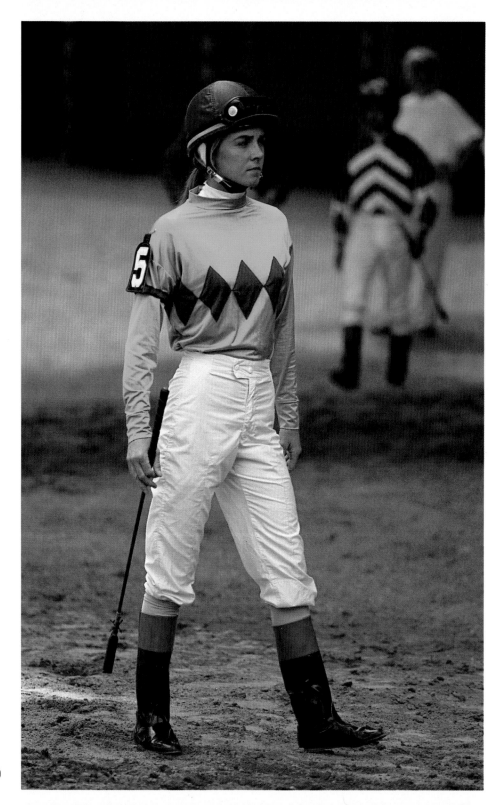

Diane Nelson

Big Red Spring

Entering the walking ring

Steeplechase race (*overleaf*)

The paddock crowd, Alfred Vanderbilt and Sheryl Schwartz

Beneath the jump

Sartaoga steeplechase

Heading to the post

The field leans into the clubhouse turn

Cutting horse competition at the Oklahoma Track

Separating a calf from the herd

Rearing in the starting gate (*overleaf*)

Kissin Kris in the walking ring

Track conditions, "Muddy"

Java Gold wins the 1987 Travers in a driving rainstorm.

An umbrella kind of day

Mike Venezia smiles through a face caked with mud.

Venezia died in a riding accident at Belmont Park on October 13,1988.

A trailer full of gear at a horse show, Skidmore College

St Clement's horse show, Schooling jumper class

Marylou Whitney with Marla and Donald Trump
at the annual Whitney Ball, 1995

Unicorns? The theme of the annual Whitney Ball held at the Canfield Casino, 1993

Travers Day hat

Arriving with style at the Gideon Putnam Hotel, Saratoga Spa State Park

High Goal Polo Match, Saratoga Polo Association

Apartment 35C versus Cold Comfort

Jockey statues, with silks painted to match the grade I stakes winners from the previous year's meet

Heading to the track for the race

Waiting their turn, St. Clement's Horse Show

Dressage competition at the Racecourse, Conquistador attire

Heading for the sale

Fasig-Tipton Yearling Sale

Fourstardave, a winner for eight consecutive years, heads toward the winner's circle with Richard Migliore up.

Holy Bull, winner of the 1994 Travers Stakes

Forty Niner, right, wins the 1988 Travers Stakes

Hall of Famers, Jerry Bailey, and MacK. Miller, trainer

They're off

Oklahoma Track in the early morning

Hot bath on a cool morning

Excercise riders at the Oklahoma Track

After the workout bath

Go For Wand, Alabama Stakes winner, 1990

Up The Apalachee (right) wins the Alabama in 1987

Around the turn on the Mellon Turf Course

Clearing the fence

Aerial view of the race course looking toward Saratoga Lake

Autumn clouds at the raceway

Stretch run at Saratoga Raceway

Schooling at the Skidmore College stables *(overleᴄ*

Photo finish

Harness race start *(overleaf)*

Jorge Chavez

Julie Krone, the top female rider

Carriages ride along Saratoga Lake

Breakfast, a race course tradition

The Hooper Barn

Freshly cleaned saddles

Charles "Shug" McGaughey, trainer for the Phipps stable

Claire Court at the backstretch of the race course

Hot walker

Neck and neck down the stretch

The clubhouse turn

D. Wayne Lucas, one of racing's most successful trainers

Thunder Gulch (left) moves to the front to win the 1995 Travers

Annual dog show at the race course

"Spirit of Saratoga," Hat Day Contest winner

Mike Smith, Saratoga riding champion
1991, 1992, and 1993

Spider's web in the morning light

A blur of speed

Pat Day brings Unaccounted For to the winner's circle in the 1995 Whitney Stakes

Silks' room, through the window

Winter morning at Saratoga Raceway

Infield canoe painted the colors of the Travers Stakes winner

Race course blanketed in snow

Paddock sign

Acknowledgements

This book would not have been possible without the assistance, support, and cooperation of many people.

Publisher, Steve Buckley, allowed me to use work published in The Record newspapers and endorsed the project from its inception.

My colleagues at The Record, Lisa Robert Lewis, managing editor, Mike McMahon, chief photographer, and photographers Jim Carras, Jeff Couch, and Susan B. Cummings lent me every assistance. I am privileged to work with such a talented group of dedicated professionals.

The team at Ed Lewi Associates Public Relations and Marketing, including Ed, his wife, Maureen and my former editor, Kathy Condon, advised and assisted me in many ways.

The New York Racing Association's Media Relations office provided invaluable assistance every year I covered the Saratoga meet.

Sid Brown, photographer and man of many talents, flew me over Saratoga Springs to do the aerial photographs.

Cynthia Ford, director of the Skidmore College Riding Program, cooperated and assisted me in photographing at the college's riding stables.

Bob Morrison, track photographer at the harness track, guided me in photographing the pacers and trotters.

Dave Murphy, of the law firm Cusick, Hacker and Murphy, provided all legal advice and assistance.

Bob Rubin supported the project from its earliest stages and provided the vital distribution network for the book.

This book would not have been possible without the vision and commitment of Ray Burke, president & CEO of Horowitz/Rae. The talented and dedicated people at Horowitz/Rae Book Manufacturers brought this collection of photographs to life with the finest attention to detail.

I am truly fortunate to have not only a supportive, but remarkably talented family. My wife, Deborah, helped design the book and provided its title. My brothers-in-law, Matt and John LaClair, helped me haul equipment and trigger remote cameras every year during the thoroughbred meet.